The Illustrated Book
of Romantic Verse

Publisher and Creative Director: Nick Wells
Project Editor and Picture Research: Esme Chapman
Special thanks to Laura Bulbeck, Emma Chafer
and Catherine Taylor

This edition first published 2014 by
FLAME TREE PUBLISHING
Crabtree Hall, Crabtree Lane
Fulham, London SW6 6TY
United Kingdom

www.flametreepublishing.com

14 16 18 17 15
3 5 7 9 10 8 6 4 2

© 2014 Flame Tree Publishing Ltd

ISBN 978-1-78361-110-2

Printed in China

The Illustrated Book of Romantic Verse

A special selection edited by E. A Chapman

**FLAME TREE
PUBLISHING**

Contents

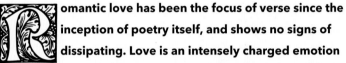

Introduction

Romantic love has been the focus of verse since the inception of poetry itself, and shows no signs of dissipating. Love is an intensely charged emotion that forces expression in its most raw and potent form. From the height of elation to the depths of heartbreak, love inspires polar opposites as well as all the shades in between. Love's guises are so convincing that the identification of love itself has become a substantial component of romantic poetry. It is a task that has been undertaken by Elizabeth Barrett Browning (1806-61), amongst others. Her poem 'Love' concerns itself with the ways in which both men and women view eternal love, attempting to uncover its vagaries and establish how this emotion can cause both such joy and such inconsolable pain.

Beginning with a section on 'Lost Love and Remembrance' which highlights the longevity of love even when it is no longer physically present, this anthology brings together the work of staple literary figures ranging from sixteenth-century writers such as William Shakespeare (1564-1616) to the works of Romanticism's pioneers, Percy Bysshe Shelley (1792-1822) and Lord Byron (1788-1824). Christina Georgina Rossetti (1830-94), also makes a substantial contribution to this collection with her poignant work. Her poem

'Remember' is haunting in its beauty as the protagonist selflessly encourages her lover not to grieve for her once she has passed away.

Despite the heartbreak that comes from such lost love, the very fact that men and women the world over continue to set their sights on finding true love is a testimony to the incomparable consumption of this emotion. Whether it be the first flurries of possibility or the depth of knowing that you have been touched by a life-changing love, such feelings are hard to beat and often even harder to eloquently express. Overcoming this difficulty, poets ranging from John Donne (1572-1631) through to W.B. Yeats (1865-1939) do justice to the inspiring power of love in the 'Uplifting Love' section.

In some cases, even given the best of intentions, the path of love does not run smooth. Whether it be a case of unrequited love, cold feet or simply missed opportunity, the section on 'Unfulfilled Love' offers words which many will identify with. From 'Love in the Guise of Friendship' by Robert Burns (1759-96) to 'Never Seek to Tell Thy Love' by William Blake (1757-1827), there are inspired words which may offer consolation and comfort to those in the throes of unfulfilled love.

Through a section dedicated to 'The Romance of Nature', this anthology concludes by exploring the ability of the natural world to evoke feelings of joy, wonder and possibility which, in many ways, parallel the elation of love. Romantic poets such as Samuel Taylor

Coleridge (1772-1834) and William Wordsworth (1770-1850) are famous for expressing their definitions of beauty though their experiences with, and observations of, nature. Such reverence for the glory of the natural world is also a reminder that as all-consuming as the grief or clutch of love may be, we remain part of a more powerful and ever-enduring environment whose existence was here before those feelings first began to stir, and will persist long after our great loves and our very lives have eclipsed.

From across the centuries, this anthology delivers poetry spanning the gamut of love's emotions in an attempt to encapsulate love's beautiful and treacherous journey, wherever you may be on it.

Lost Love and Remembrance 🍃

Stanzas
("Oh, come to me in dreams, my love!")
Mary Wollstonecraft Shelley (1759–97)

Oh, come to me in dreams, my love!
I will not ask a dearer bliss;
Come with the starry beams, my love,
And press mine eyelids with thy kiss.

'Twas thus, as ancient fables tell,
Love visited a Grecian maid,
Till she disturbed the sacred spell,
And woke to find her hopes betrayed.

But gentle sleep shall veil my sight,
And Psyche's lamp shall darkling be,
When, in the visions of the night,
Thou dost renew thy vows to me.

Then come to me in dreams, my love,
I will not ask a dearer bliss;
Come with the starry beams, my love,
And press mine eyelids with thy kiss.

I Hid My Love
John Clare (1793–1864)

I hid my love when young till I
Couldn't bear the buzzing of a fly;
I hid my love to my despite
Till I could not bear to look at light:
I dare not gaze upon her face
But left her memory in each place;
Where'er I saw a wild flower lie
I kissed and bade my love good-bye.

I met her in the greenest dells,
Where dewdrops pearl the wood bluebells;
The lost breeze kissed her bright blue eye,
The bee kissed and went singing by,
A sunbeam found a passage there,
A gold chain round her neck so fair;
As secret as the wild bee's song
She lay there all the summer long.

I hid my love in field and town
Till e'en the breeze would knock me down;
The bees seemed singing ballads o'er,
The fly's bass turned a lion's roar;
And even silence found a tongue,
To haunt me all the summer long;
The riddle nature could not prove
Was nothing else but secret love.

When We Two Parted

George Gordon, Lord Byron (1788–1824)

When we two parted
In silence and tears,
Half broken-hearted
To sever for years,
Pale grew thy cheek and cold,
Colder thy kiss;
Truly that hour foretold
Sorrow to this.

The dew of the morning
Sunk chill on my brow –
It felt like the warning
Of what I feel now.
Thy vows are all broken,
And light is thy fame;
I hear thy name spoken,
And share in its shame.

They name thee before me,
A knell to mine ear;
A shudder comes o'er me –
Why wert thou so dear?
They know not I knew thee,
Who knew thee too well:
Long, long shall I rue thee,
Too deeply to tell.

In secret we met –
In silence I grieve,
That thy heart could forget,
Thy spirit deceive.
If I should meet thee
After long years,
How should I greet thee?
With silence and tears.

Maid of Athens, Ere We Part

George Gordon, Lord Byron (1788–1824)

Maid of Athens, ere we part,
Give, oh give me back my heart!
Or, since that has left my breast,
Keep it now, and take the rest!
Hear my vow before I go,
Zoë mou, sas agapo!

By those tresses unconfined,
Wooed by each Aegean wind;
By those lids whose jetty fringe
Kiss thy soft cheeks' blooming tinge;
By those wild eyes like the roe,
Zoë mou, sas agapo!

By that lip I long to taste;
By that zone-encircled waist;
By all the token-flowers that tell
What words can never speak so well;
By love's alternate joy and woe.
Zoë mou, sas agapo!

Maid of Athens! I am gone:
Think of me, sweet! when alone.
Though I fly to Istambol,
Athens holds my heart and soul:
Can I cease to love thee? No!
Zoë mou, sas agapo!

So, We'll Go No More A Roving

George Gordon, Lord Byron (1788–1824)

I

So, We'll go no more a roving
So late into the night,
Though the heart be still as loving,
And the moon be still as bright.

II

For the sword outwears its sheath,
And the soul wears out the breast,
And the heart must pause to breathe,
And love itself have rest.

III

Though the night was made for loving,
And the day returns too soon,
Yet we'll go no more a roving
By the light of the moon.

Ephemera
W.B. Yeats (1865–1939)

'Your eyes that once were never weary of mine
Are bowed in sorrow under pendulous lids,
Because our love is waning.'
And then she:
'Although our love is waning, let us stand
By the lone border of the lake once more,
Together in that hour of gentleness
When the poor tired child, Passion, falls asleep.
How far away the stars seem, and how far
Is our first kiss, and ah, how old my heart!'

Pensive they paced along the faded leaves,
While slowly he whose hand held hers replied:
'Passion has often worn our wandering hearts.'

The woods were round them, and the yellow leaves
Fell like faint meteors in the gloom, and once
A rabbit old and lame limped down the path;
Autumn was over him: and now they stood
On the lone border of the lake once more:
Turning, he saw that she had thrust dead leaves
Gathered in silence, dewy as her eyes,
In bosom and hair.

'Ah, do not mourn,' he said,
'That we are tired, for other loves await us;
Hate on and love through unrepining hours.
Before us lies eternity; our souls
Are love, and a continual farewell.'

The Lover Tells of the Rose in his Heart
W.B. Yeats (1865–1939)

All things uncomely and broken, all things worn out and old,
The cry of a child by the roadway, the creak of a lumbering cart,
The heavy steps of the ploughman, splashing the wintry mould,
Are wronging your image that blossoms a rose in the deeps of my heart.

The wrong of unshapely things is a wrong too great to be told;
I hunger to build them anew and sit on a green knoll apart,
With the earth and the sky and the water, re-made, like a casket of gold
For my dreams of your image that blossoms a rose in the deeps of my heart.

A Woman Homer Sung
W.B. Yeats (1865–1939)

If any man drew near
When I was young,
I thought, 'He holds her dear,'
And shook with hate and fear.
But O! 'twas bitter wrong
If he could pass her by
With an indifferent eye.

Whereon I wrote and wrought,
And now, being grey,
I dream that I have brought
To such a pitch my thought
That coming time can say,
'He shadowed in a glass
What thing her body was.'

For she had fiery blood
When I was young,
And trod so sweetly proud
As 'twere upon a cloud,
A woman Homer sung,
That life and letters seem
But an heroic dream.

The Winter it is Past

Robert Burns (1759–96)

The winter it is past, and the summer comes at last
And the small birds sing on ev'ry tree;
The hearts of these are glad, but mine is very sad,
For my love is parted from me.

The rose upon the brier by the waters running clear
May have charms for the linnet or the bee:
Their little loves are blest, and their little hearts at rest,
But my lover is parted from me.

My love is like the sun
And the firmament does run -
Forever is constant and true;
But his is like the moon, that wanders up and down,
And every month it is new.

All you that are in love, and cannot it remove,
I pity the pains you endure,
For experience makes me know that your hearts are full of woe,
A woe that no mortal can cure.

Annabel Lee
Edgar Allan Poe (1809–49)

It was many and many a year ago,
In a kingdom by the sea,
That a maiden there lived whom you may know
By the name of Annabel Lee;
And this maiden she lived with no other thought
Than to love and be loved by me.

I was a child and she was a child,
In this kingdom by the sea;
But we loved with a love that was more than love
I and my Annabel Lee;
With a love that the wingèd seraphs of Heaven
Coveted her and me.

And this was the reason that, long ago,
In this kingdom by the sea,
A wind blew out of a cloud, chilling
My beautiful Annabel Lee;
So that her high-born kinsmen came
And bore her away from me,
To shut her up in a sepulchre,
In this kingdom by the sea.

The angels, not half so happy in Heaven,
Went envying her and me...
Yes! that was the reason (as all men know,
In this kingdom by the sea)
That the wind came out of the cloud by night,
Chilling and killing my Annabel Lee.

But our love it was stronger by far than the love
Of those who were older than we,
Of many far wiser than we
And neither the angels in Heaven above,
Nor the demons down under the sea,
Can ever dissever my soul from the soul
Of the beautiful Annabel Lee,

For the moon never beams, without bringing me dreams
Of the beautiful Annabel Lee;
And the stars never rise, but I feel the bright eyes
Of the beautiful Annabel Lee;
And so, all the night-tide, I lie down by the side
Of my darling, my darling, my life and my bride,
In her sepulchre there by the sea,
In her tomb by the sounding sea.

The Dirge
Percy Bysshe Shelley (1792–1822)

Old winter was gone
In his weakness back to the mountains hoar,
And the spring came down
From the planet that hovers upon the shore
Where the sea of sunlight encroaches
On the limits of wintry night;
If the land, and the air, and the sea,
Rejoice not when spring approaches,
We did not rejoice in thee,
Ginevra!

She is still, she is cold
On the bridal couch,
One step to the white deathbed,
And one to the charnel – and one, Oh where?
The dark arrow fled
In the noon.

Ere the sun through heaven once more has rolled
The rats in her heart
Will have made their nest,
And the worms be alive in her golden hair;
While the spirit that guides the sun
Sits throned in his flaming chair,
She shall sleep.

Remember
Christina Rossetti (1830–94)

Remember me when I am gone away,
Gone far away into the silent land;
When you can no more hold me by the hand,
Nor I half turn to go yet turning stay.
Remember me when no more day by day
You tell me of our future that you planned:
Only remember me; you understand
It will be late to counsel then or pray.
Yet if you should forget me for a while
And afterwards remember, do not grieve:
For if the darkness and corruption leave
A vestige of the thoughts that once I had,
Better by far you should forget and smile
Than that you should remember and be sad.

A Dream
Christina Rossetti (1830–94)

Once in a dream (for once I dreamed of you)
We stood together in an open field;
Above our heads two swift-winged pigeons wheeled,
Sporting at ease and courting full in view.
When loftier still a broadening darkness flew,
Down-swooping, and a ravenous hawk revealed;
Too weak to fight, too fond to fly, they yield;
So farewell life and love and pleasures new.
Then as their plumes fell fluttering to the ground,
Their snow-white plumage flecked with crimson drops,
I wept, and thought I turned towards you to weep:
But you were gone; while rustling hedgerow tops
Bent in a wind which bore to me a sound
Of far-off piteous bleat of lambs and sheep.

One Day
Christina Rossetti (1830–94)

I will tell you when they met:
In the limpid days of Spring;
Elder boughs were budding yet,
Oaken boughs looked wintry still,
But primrose and veined violet
In the mossful turf were set,
While meeting birds made haste to sing
And build with right good will.

I will tell you when they parted:
When plenteous Autumn sheaves were brown,
Then they parted heavy-hearted;
The full rejoicing sun looked down
As grand as in the days before;
Only they had lost a crown;
Only to them those days of yore
Could come back nevermore.

When shall they meet? I cannot tell,
Indeed, when they shall meet again,
Except some day in Paradise:
For this they wait, one waits in pain.
Beyond the sea of death love lies
For ever, yesterday, to-day;
Angels shall ask them, 'Is it well?'
And they shall answer, 'Yea.'

Uplifting Love 🌿

Sonnet 18
William Shakespeare (1564–1616)

Shall I compare thee to a summer's day?
Thou art more lovely and more temperate:
Rough winds do shake the darling buds of May,
And summer's lease hath all too short a date:
Sometime too hot the eye of heaven shines,
And often is his gold complexion dimm'd;
And every fair from fair sometime declines,
By chance, or nature's changing course untrimm'd;
But thy eternal summer shall not fade,
Nor lose possession of that fair thou ow'st,
Nor shall death brag thou wander'st in his shade,
When in eternal lines to time thou grow'st;
So long as men can breathe, or eyes can see,
So long lives this, and this gives life to thee.

That Time and Absence Proves

John Donne (1572–1631)

Absence, hear thou my protestation
Against thy strength,
Distance and length:
Do what thou canst for alteration,
For hearts of truest mettle
Absence doth join and Time doth settle.

Who loves a mistress of such quality,
His mind hath found
Affection's ground
Beyond time, place, and all mortality.
To hearts that cannot vary
Absence is present, Time doth tarry.

My senses want their outward motion
Which now within
Reason doth win,
Redoubled by her secret notion:
Like rich men that take pleasure
In hiding more than handling treasure.

By Absence this good means I gain,
That I can catch her
Where none can watch her,
In some close corner of my brain:
There I embrace and kiss her,
And so enjoy her and none miss her.

Sonnet 116
William Shakespeare (1564–1616)

Let me not to the marriage of true minds
Admit impediments. Love is not love
Which alters when it alteration finds,
Or bends with the remover to remove:
O, no! it is an ever-fixed mark,
That looks on tempests and is never shaken;
It is the star to every wandering bark,
Whose worth's unknown, although his height be taken.
Love's not Time's fool, though rosy lips and cheeks
Within his bending sickle's compass come;
Love alters not with his brief hours and weeks,
But bears it out even to the edge of doom.
If this be error, and upon me prov'd,
I never writ, nor no man ever lov'd.

Air and Angels
John Donne (1572 – 1631)

Twice or thrice had I loved thee,
Before I knew thy face or name;
So in a voice, so in a shapeless flame,
Angels affect us oft, and worshipped be;
Still when, to where thou wert, I came,
Some lovely glorious nothing I did see,
But since my soul, whose child love is,
Takes limbs of flesh, and else could nothing do,
More subtle than the parent is
Love must not be, but take a body too,
And therefore what thou wert, and who
I bid love ask, and now
That it assume thy body, I allow,
And fix itself in thy lip, eye, and brow

Whilst thus to ballast love, I thought,

And so more steadily to have gone,

With wares which would sink admiration,

I saw, I had love's pinnace overfraught,

Thy every hair for love to work upon

Is too much, some fitter must be sought;

For, nor in nothing, nor in things

Extreme, and scatt'ring bright, can love inhere;

Then as an angel, face and wings

Of air, not pure as it, yet doth wear,

So thy love may be my love's sphere;

Just such disparity

As is 'twixt air and angels' purity

'Twixt women's love, and men's will ever be.

All for Love
George Gordon, Lord Byron (1788–1824)

O talk not to me of a name great in story;
The days of our youth are the days of our glory;
And the myrtle and ivy of sweet two-and-twenty
Are worth all your laurels, though ever so plenty.

What are garlands and crowns to the brow that is wrinkled?
'Tis but as a dead flower with May-dew besprinkled:
Then away with all such from the head that is hoary-
What care I for the wreaths that can only give glory?

Oh Fame! –if I e'er took delight in thy praises,
'Twas less for the sake of thy high-sounding phrases,
Than to see the bright eyes of the dear one discover
She thought that I was not unworthy to love her.

There chiefly I sought thee, there only I found thee;
Her glance was the best of the rays that surround thee;
When it sparkled o'er aught that was bright in my story,
I knew it was love, and I felt it was glory.

She Walks in Beauty
George Gordon, Lord Byron (1788–1824)

I

She walks in beauty, like the night
Of cloudless climes and starry skies;
And all that's best of dark and bright
Meet in her aspect and her eyes:
Thus mellow'd to that tender light
Which heaven to gaudy day denies.

II

One shade the more, one ray the less,
Had half impair'd the nameless grace
Which waves in every raven tress,
Or softly lightens o'er her face;
Where thoughts serenely sweet express
How pure, how dear their dwelling-place.

III

And on that cheek, and o'er that brow,
So soft, so calm, yet eloquent,
The smiles that win, the tints that glow,
But tell of days in goodness spent,
A mind at peace with all below,
A heart whose love is innocent!

When You Are Old
W. B. Yeats (1865–1939)

When you are old and grey and full of sleep,
And nodding by the fire, take down this book,
And slowly read, and dream of the soft look
Your eyes had once, and of their shadows deep;

How many loved your moments of glad grace,
And loved your beauty with love false or true,
But one man loved the pilgrim soul in you,
And loved the sorrows of your changing face;

And bending down beside the glowing bars,
Murmur, a little sadly, how Love fled
And paced upon the mountains overhead
And hid his face amid a crowd of stars.

Genevieve
Samuel Taylor Coleridge (1772–1834)

Maid of my Love, sweet Genevieve!
In Beauty's light you glide along:
Your eye is like the star of eve,
And sweet your Vice, as Seraph's song.
Yet not your heavenly Beauty gives
This heart with passion soft to glow:
Within your soul a voice there lives!
It bids you hear the tale of Woe.
When sinking low the Suff'rer wan
Beholds no hand outstretch'd to save,
Fair, as the bosom of the Swan
That rises graceful o'er the wave,
I've seen your breast with pity heave,
And therefore love I you, sweet Genevieve!

Afton Water
Robert Burns (1759–96)

Flow gently, sweet Afton, among thy green braes,
Flow gently, I'll sing thee a song in thy praise;
My Mary's asleep by thy murmuring stream,
Flow gently, sweet Afton, disturb not her dream.

Thou stock-dove, whose echo resounds thro' the glen,
Ye wild whistling blackbirds in yon thorny den,
Thou green-crested lapwing, thy screaming forbear,
I charge you disturb not my slumbering fair.

How lofty, sweet Afton, thy neighbouring hills,
Far mark'd with the courses of clear winding rills;
There daily I wander as noon rises high,
My flocks and my Mary's sweet cot in my eye.

How pleasant thy banks and green valleys below,
Where wild in the woodlands the primroses blow;
There oft, as mild Ev'ning sweeps over the lea,
The sweet-scented birk shades my Mary and me.

Thy crystal stream, Afton, how lovely it glides,
And winds by the cot where my Mary resides,
How wanton thy waters her snowy feet lave,
As gathering sweet flowrets she stems thy clear wave.

Flow gently, sweet Afton, among thy green braes,
Flow gently, sweet river, the theme of my lays;
My Mary's asleep by thy murmuring stream,
Flow gently, sweet Afton, disturb not her dream.

To Jane
Percy Bysshe Shelley (1792–1822)

The keen stars were twinkling,
And the fair moon was rising among them,
Dear Jane!
The guitar was tinkling,
But the notes were not sweet till you sung them
Again.

As the moon's soft splendour
O'er the faint cold starlight of Heaven
Is thrown,
So your voice most tender
To the strings without soul had then given
Its own.

The stars will awaken,
Though the moon sleep a full hour later,
To-night;
No leaf will be shaken
Whilst the dews of your melody scatter
Delight.

Though the sound overpowers,
Sing again, with your dear voice revealing
A tone
Of some world far from ours,
Where music and moonlight and feeling
Are one.

Love
Elizabeth Barrett Browning (1806–61)

We cannot live, except thus mutually
We alternate, aware or unaware,
The reflex act of life; and when we bear
Our virtue outward most impulsively,
Most full of invocation, and to be
Most instantly compellent, certes, there
We live most life, whoever breathes most air,
And counts his dying years by sun and sea.
But when a soul, by choice and conscience, doth
Throw out her full force on another soul,
The conscience and the concentration both
Make mere life, Love. For Life in perfect whole
And aim consummated, is love in sooth,
As nature's magnet-heat rounds pole with pole.

First Love
John Clare (1793–1864)

I ne'er was struck before that hour
With love so sudden and so sweet,
Her face it bloomed like a sweet flower
And stole my heart away complete.
My face turned pale as deadly pale.
My legs refused to walk away,
And when she looked, what could I ail?
My life and all seemed turned to clay.

And then my blood rushed to my face
And took my eyesight quite away,
The trees and bushes round the place
Seemed midnight at noonday.
I could not see a single thing,
Words from my eyes did start –
They spoke as chords do from the string,
And blood burnt round my heart.

Are flowers the winter's choice?
Is love's bed always snow?
She seemed to hear my silent voice,
Not love's appeals to know.
I never saw so sweet a face
As that I stood before.
My heart has left its dwelling-place
And can return no more.

A Valentine
Edgar Allan Poe (1809–1849)

For her this rhyme is penned, whose luminous eyes,

Brightly expressive as the twins of Leda,

Shall find her own sweet name, that nestling lies

Upon the page, enwrapped from every reader.

Search narrowly the lines!- they hold a treasure

Divine- a talisman- an amulet

That must be worn at heart. Search well the measure-

The words- the syllables! Do not forget

The trivialest point, or you may lose your labor

And yet there is in this no Gordian knot

Which one might not undo without a sabre,

If one could merely comprehend the plot.

Enwritten upon the leaf where now are peering

Eyes scintillating soul, there lie perdus

Three eloquent words oft uttered in the hearing

Of poets, by poets- as the name is a poet's, too,

Its letters, although naturally lying

Like the knight Pinto- Mendez Ferdinando-

Still form a synonym for Truth- Cease trying!

You will not read the riddle, though you do the best you can do.

The First Kiss of Love
George Gordon, Lord Byron (1788–1824)

Away with your fictions of flimsy romance;
Those tissues of falsehood which folly has wove!
Give me the mild beam of the soul-breathing glance,
Or the rapture which dwells on the first kiss of love.

Ye rhymers, whose bosoms with phantasy glow,
Whose pastoral passions are made for the grove;
From what blest inspiration your sonnets would flow,
Could you ever have tasted the first kiss of love!

If Apollo should e'er his assistance refuse,
Or the Nine be disposed from your service to rove,
Invoke them no more, bid adieu to the muse,
And try the effect of the first kiss of love.

I hate you, ye cold compositions of art!
Though prudes may condemn me, and bigots reprove,
I court the effusions that spring from the heart,
Which throbs with delight to the first kiss of love.

Your shepherds, your flocks, those fantastical themes,
Perhaps may amuse, yet they never can move:
Arcadia displays but a region of dreams:
What are visions like these to the first kiss of love?

Oh! cease to affirm that man, since his birth,
From Adam till now, has with wretchedness strove,
Some portion of paradise still is on earth,
And Eden revives in the first kiss of love.

When age chills the blood, when our pleasures are past –
For years fleet away with the wings of the dove –
The dearest remembrance will still be the last,
Our sweetest memorial the first kiss of love.

Ah, How Sweet it is to Love
John Dryden (1631–1700)

Ah, how sweet it is to love!
Ah, how gay is young Desire!
And what pleasing pains we prove
When we first approach Love's fire!
Pains of love be sweeter far
Than all other pleasures are.

Sighs which are from lovers blown
Do but gently heave the heart:
Ev'n the tears they shed alone
Cure, like trickling balm, their smart:
Lovers, when they lose their breath,
Bleed away in easy death.
Love and Time with reverence use,
Treat them like a parting friend;
Nor the golden gifts refuse
Which in youth sincere they send:
For each year their price is more,
And they less simple than before.

Love, like spring-tides full and high,
Swells in every youthful vein;
But each tide does less supply,
Till they quite shrink in again:
If a flow in age appear,
'Tis but rain, and runs not clear.

O Mistress Mine

William Shakespeare (1564–1616)

O Mistress mine, where are you roaming?
O stay and hear! your true-love's coming
That can sing both high and low;
Trip no further, pretty sweeting,
Journeys end in lovers' meeting-
Every wise man's son doth know.

What is love? 'tis not hereafter;
Present mirth hath present laughter;
What's to come is still unsure:
In delay there lies no plenty,-
Then come kiss me, Sweet-and-twenty,
Youth's a stuff will not endure.

Unfulfilled Love 🌿

J.W. GODWARD 1901.

Love in the Guise of Friendship
Robert Burns (1759–96)

Talk not of love, it gives me pain,
For love has been my foe;
He bound me in an iron chain,
And plung'd me deep in woe.

But friendship's pure and lasting joys,
My heart was form'd to prove;
There, welcome win and wear the prize,
But never talk of love.

Your friendship much can make me blest,
O why that bliss destroy?
Why urge the only, one request
You know I will deny?

Your thought, if Love must harbour there,
Conceal it in that thought;
Nor cause me from my bosom tear
The very friend I sought.

Never Seek to Tell Thy Love
William Blake (1757 – 1827)

Never seek to tell thy love,
Love that never told can be;
For the gentle wind does move
Silently, invisibly.

I told my love, I told my love.
I told her all my heart,
Trembling, cold, in ghastly fears
Ah, she doth depart.

Soon as she was gone from me
A traveler came by
Silently, invisibly
He took her with a sigh. O, was no deny.

A Dream Within A Dream

Edgar Allan Poe (1809–1849)

Take this kiss upon the brow!

And, in parting from you now,

Thus much let me avow-

You are not wrong, who deem

That my days have been a dream;

Yet if hope has flown away

In a night, or in a day,

In a vision, or in none,

Is it therefore the less gone?

All that we see or seem

Is but a dream within a dream.

I stand amid the roar

Of a surf-tormented shore,

And I hold within my hand

Grains of the golden sand-

How few! yet how they creep

Through my fingers to the deep,

While I weep- while I weep!

O God! can I not grasp

Them with a tighter clasp?

O God! can I not save

One from the pitiless wave?

Is all that we see or seem

But a dream within a dream?

The Presence of Love
Samuel Taylor Coleridge (1772–1834)

And in Life's noisiest hour,
There whispers still the ceaseless Love of Thee,
The heart's Self-solace and soliloquy.

You mould my Hopes, you fashion me within;
And to the leading Love-throb in the Heart
Thro' all my Being, thro' my pulses beat;
You lie in all my many Thoughts, like Light,
Like the fair light of Dawn, or summer Eve
On rippling Stream, or cloud-reflecting Lake.

And looking to the Heaven, that bends above you,
How oft! I bless the Lot, that made me love you.

Sonnet 137
William Shakespeare (1564–1616)

Thou blind fool, Love, what dost thou to mine eyes
That they behold, and see not what they see?
They know what beauty is, see where it lies,
Yet what the best is take the worst to be.
If eyes, corrupt by over-partial looks,
Be anchor'd in the bay where all men ride,
Why of eyes' falsehood hast thou forged hooks,
Whereto the judgment of my heart is tied?
Why should, my heart think that a several plot,
Which my heart knows the wide world's common place?
Or mine eyes, seeing this, say this is not,
To put fair truth upon so foul a face?
In things right true my heart and eyes have erred,
And to this false plague are they now transferred.

Down By The Salley Gardens
W.B. Yeats (1865–1939)

Down by the salley gardens my love and I did meet;
She passed the salley gardens with little snow-white feet.
She bid me take love easy, as the leaves grow on the tree;
But I, being young and foolish, with her would not agree.

In a field by the river my love and I did stand,
And on my leaning shoulder she laid her snow-white hand.
She bid me take life easy, as the grass grows on the weirs;
But I was young and foolish, and now am full of tears.

The Solitary Reaper
William Wordsworth (1770–1850)

Behold her, single in the field,
You solitary Highland Lass!
Reaping and singing by herself;
Stop here, or gently pass!
Alone she cuts and binds the grain,
And sings a melancholy strain;
O listen! for the Vale profound
Is overflowing with the sound.

No Nightingale did ever chaunt
More welcome notes to weary bands
Of travellers in some shady haunt,
Among Arabian sands:
A voice so thrilling ne'er was heard
In spring-time from the Cuckoo-bird,
Breaking the silence of the seas
Among the farthest Hebrides.
Will no one tell me what she sings?

The Exchange
Samuel Taylor Coleridge (1772–1834)

We pledged our hearts, my love and I, –
I in my arms the maiden clasping;
I could not guess the reason why,
But, oh! I trembled like an aspen.

Her father's love she bade me gain;
I went, but shook like any reed!
I strove to act the man – in vain!
We had exchanges our hearts indeed.

Handsome Nell
Robert Burns (1759–96)

O Once I lov'd a bonnie lass,
An' aye I love her still,
An' whilst that virtue warms my breast
I'll love my handsome Nell.

As bonnie lasses I hae seen,
And mony full as braw;
But for a modest gracefu' mein,
The like I never saw.

A bonny lass I will confess,
Is pleasant to the e'e,
But without some better qualities
She's no a lass for me.

But Nelly's looks are blythe and sweet,
And what is best of a',
Her reputation is compleat,
And fair without a flaw;

She dresses aye sae clean and neat,
Both decent and genteel;
And then there's something in her gait
Gars ony dress look weel.

A gaudy dress and gentle air
May slightly touch the heart,
But it's innocence and modesty
That polishes the dart.

'Tis this in Nelly pleases me,
'Tis this enchants my soul;
For absolutely in my breast
She reigns without control.

Mary Morison (A Song)
Robert Burns (1759–96)

O Mary, at thy window be,
It is the wish'd, the trysted hour!
Those smiles and glances let me see,
That make the miser's treasure poor:
How blythely was I bide the stour,
A weary slave frae sun to sun,
Could I the rich reward secure,
The lovely Mary Morison.

Yestreen, when to the trembling string
The dance gaed thro' the lighted ha',
To thee my fancy took its wing,
I sat, but neither heard nor saw:
Tho' this was fair, and that was braw,
And yon the toast of a' the town,
I sigh'd, and said among them a',
"Ye are na Mary Morison."

Oh, Mary, canst thou wreck his peace,
Wha for thy sake wad gladly die?
Or canst thou break that heart of his,
Whase only faut is loving thee?
If love for love thou wilt na gie,
At least be pity to me shown;
A thought ungentle canna be
The thought o' Mary Morison.

Lines – When the Lamp is Shattered

Percy Bysshe Shelley (1792–1822)

When the lamp is shattered
The light in the dust lies dead—
When the cloud is scattered
The rainbow's glory is shed.
When the lute is broken,
Sweet tones are remembered not;
When the lips have spoken,
Loved accents are soon forgot.

As music and splendor
Survive not the lamp and the lute,
The heart's echoes render
No song when the spirit is mute:—
No song but sad dirges,
Like the wind through a ruined cell,
Or the mournful surges
That ring the dead seaman's knell.

When hearts have once mingled
Love first leaves the well-built nest;
The weak one is singled
To endure what it once possessed.
O Love! who bewailest
The frailty of all things here,
Why choose you the frailest
For your cradle, your home, and your bier?

Its passions will rock thee
As the storms rock the ravens on high;
Bright reason will mock thee,
Like the sun from a wintry sky.
From thy nest every rafter
Will rot, and thine eagle home
Leave thee naked to laughter,
When leaves fall and cold winds come.

A Triad
Christina Rossetti (1830–94)

Three sang of love together: one with lips
Crimson, with cheeks and bosom in a glow,
Flushed to the yellow hair and finger-tips;
And one there sang who soft and smooth as snow
Bloomed like a tinted hyacinth at a show;
And one was blue with famine after love,
Who like a harpstring snapped rang harsh and low
The burden of what those were singing of.
One shamed herself in love; one temperately
Grew gross in soulless love, a sluggish wife;
One famished died for love. Thus two of three
Took death for love and won him after strife;
One droned in sweetness like a fattened bee:
All on the threshold, yet all short of life.

On Finding a Fan
George Gordon, Lord Byron (1788–1824)

In one who felt as once he felt,
This might, perhaps, have fann'd the flame;
But now his heart no more will melt,
Because that heart is not the same.

As when the ebbing flames are low,
The aid which once improved their light,
And bade them burn with fiercer glow,
Now quenches all their blaze in night.

Thus has it been with passion's fires–
As many a boy and girl remembers –
While every hope of love expires,
Extinguish'd with thy dying embers.

The first, though not a spark survive,
Some careful hand may teach to burn;
The last, alas! can ne'er survive;
No touch can bid its warmth return

Or, if it chance to wake again,
Not always doom'd its heat to smother,
It sheds (so wayward fates ordain)
Its former warmth around another.

The Romance
of Nature 🖋

Romance
Edgar Allan Poe (1809–1849)

Romance, who loves to nod and sing,
With drowsy head and folded wing,
Among the green leaves as they shake
Far down within some shadowy lake,
To me a painted paroquet
Hath been—a most familiar bird—
Taught me my alphabet to say—
To lisp my very earliest word
While in the wild wood I did lie,
A child—with a most knowing eye.

Of late, eternal Condor years
So shake the very Heaven on high
With tumult as they thunder by,
I have no time for idle cares
Through gazing on the unquiet sky.
And when an hour with calmer wings
Its down upon my spirit flings—
That little time with lyre and rhyme
To while away—forbidden things!
My heart would feel to be a crime
Unless it trembled with the strings.

The Garden of Love
William Blake (1757–1827)

I laid me down upon a bank,
Where Love lay sleeping;
I heard among the rushes dank
Weeping, weeping.

Then I went to the heath and the wild,
To the thistles and thorns of the waste;
And they told me how they were beguiled,
Driven out, and compelled to the chaste.

I went to the Garden of Love,
And saw what I never had seen:
A Chapel was built in the midst,
Where I used to play on the green.

And the gates of this Chapel were shut,
And 'Thou shalt not,' writ over the door;
So I turned to the Garden of Love
That so many sweet flowers bore.

And I saw it was filled with graves,
And tombstones where flowers should be:
And priests in black gowns, were walking their rounds,
And binding with briars my joys & desires.

Love's Philosophy
Percy Bysshe Shelley (1792–1822)

The fountains mingle with the river
And the rivers with the ocean,
The winds of heaven mix for ever
With a sweet emotion;
Nothing in the world is single,
All things by a law divine
In one another's being mingle–
Why not I with thine?

See the mountains kiss high heaven,
And the waves clasp one another;
No sister-flower would be forgiven
If it disdain'd its brother;
And the sunlight clasps the earth,
And the moonbeams kiss the sea–
What are all these kissings worth,
If thou kiss not me?

On the Grasshopper and Cricket
John Keats (1795–1821)

The poetry of earth is never dead:
When all the birds are faint with the hot sun,
And hide in cooling trees, a voice will run
From hedge to hedge about the new-mown mead –
That is the Grasshopper's. He takes the lead
In summer luxury; he has never done
With his delights, for when tired out with fun
He rests at ease beneath some pleasant weed.
The poetry of earth is ceasing never:
On a lone winter evening, when the frost
Has wrought a silence, from the stove there shrills
The Cricket's song, in warmth increasing ever,
And seems to one in drowsiness half lost,
The Grasshopper's among some grassy hills.

Happy is England! I could be content

John Keats (1795–1821)

Happy is England! I could be content
To see no other verdure than its own;
To feel no other breezes than are blown
Through its tall woods with high romances blent;
Yet I do sometimes feel a languishment
For skies Italian, and an inward groan
To sit upon an Alp as on a throne,
And half forget what world or worldling meant.
Happy is England, sweet her artless daughters;
Enough their simple loveliness for me,
Enough their whitest arms in silence clinging:
Yet do I often warmly burn to see
Beauties of deeper glance, and hear their singing,
And float with them about the summer waters.

To Autumn
John Keats (1795–1821)

Season of mists and mellow fruitfulness,
Close bosom-friend of the maturing sun,
Conspiring with him how to load and bless
With fruit the vines that round the thatch-eves run;
To bend with apples the mossed cottage-trees,
And fill all fruit with ripeness to the core;
To swell the gourd, and plump the hazel shells
With a sweet kernel; to set budding more,
And still more, later flowers for the bees,
Until they think warm days will never cease,
For Summer has o'er-brimmed their clammy cells.

Who hath not seen thee oft amid thy store?
Sometimes whoever seeks abroad may find
Thee sitting careless on a granary floor,
Thy hair soft-lined by the winnowing wind;
Or on a half-reaped furrow sound asleep,

Drowsed with the fume of poppies, while thy hook
Spares the next swath and all its twined flowers;
And sometimes like a gleaner thou dost keep
Steady thy laden head across a brook;
Or by a cider-press, with patient look,
Thou watchest the last oozings hours by hours.

Where are the songs of Spring? Ay, where are they?
Think not of them, thou hast thy music too –
While barred clouds bloom the soft-dying day,
And touch the stubble-plains with rosy hue:
Then in a wailful choir the small gnats mourn
Among the river sallows, borne aloft
Or sinking as the light wind lives or dies;
And full-grown lambs loud bleat from hilly bourn;
Hedge-crickets sing; and now with treble soft
The red-breast whistles from a garden-croft;
And gathering swallows twitter in the skies.

The Wild Swans at Coole
W. B. Yeats (1865–1939)

The trees are in their autumn beauty,
The woodland paths are dry,
Under the October twilight the water
Mirrors a still sky;
Upon the brimming water among the stones
Are nine-and-fifty swans.

The nineteenth autumn has come upon me
Since I first made my count;
I saw, before I had well finished,
All suddenly mount
And scatter wheeling in great broken rings
Upon their clamorous wings.

I have looked upon those brilliant creatures,
And now my heart is sore.
All's changed since I, hearing at twilight,
The first time on this shore,
The bell-beat of their wings above my head,
Trod with a lighter tread.

Unwearied still, lover by lover,
They paddle in the cold
Companionable streams or climb the air;
Their hearts have not grown old;
Passion or conquest, wander where they will,
Attend upon them still.

But now they drift on the still water,
Mysterious, beautiful;
Among what rushes will they build,
By what lake's edge or pool
Delight men's eyes when I awake some day
To find they have flown away?

Coole Park, 1929
W. B. Yeats (1865 – 1939)

I meditate upon a swallow's flight,
Upon a aged woman and her house,
A sycamore and lime-tree lost in night
Although that western cloud is luminous,
Great works constructed there in nature's spite
For scholars and for poets after us,
Thoughts long knitted into a single thought,
A dance-like glory that those walls begot.

There Hyde before he had beaten into prose
That noble blade the Muses buckled on,
There one that ruffled in a manly pose
For all his timid heart, there that slow man,
That meditative man, John Synge, and those
Impetuous men, Shawe-Taylor and Hugh Lane,
Found pride established in humility,
A scene well Set and excellent company.

They came like swallows and like swallows went,
And yet a woman's powerful character
Could keep a Swallow to its first intent;
And half a dozen in formation there,
That seemed to whirl upon a compass-point,
Found certainty upon the dreaming air,
The intellectual sweetness of those lines
That cut through time or cross it withershins.

Here, traveller, scholar, poet, take your stand
When all those rooms and passages are gone,
When nettles wave upon a shapeless mound
And saplings root among the broken stone,
And dedicate - eyes bent upon the ground,
Back turned upon the brightness of the sun
And all the sensuality of the shade -
A moment's memory to that laurelled head.

I wandered Lonely as a Cloud
William Wordsworth (1770–1850)

I wandered lonely as a cloud
That floats on high o'er vales and hills,
When all at once I saw a crowd,
A host, of golden daffodils;
Beside the lake, beneath the trees,
Fluttering and dancing in the breeze.

Continuous as the stars that shine
And twinkle on the milky way,
They stretched in never-ending line
Along the margin of a bay:
Ten thousand saw I at a glance,
Tossing their heads in sprightly dance.

The waves beside them danced; but they
Out-did the sparkling waves in glee:
A poet could not but be gay,
In such a jocund company:
I gazed—and gazed—but little thought
What wealth the show to me had brought:

For oft, when on my couch I lie
In vacant or in pensive mood,
They flash upon that inward eye
Which is the bliss of solitude;
And then my heart with pleasure fills,
And dances with the daffodils.

To the Nightingale
Samuel Taylor Coleridge (1772–1834)

Sister of love-lorn Poets, Philomel!
How many Bards in city garret pent,
While at their window they with downward eye
Mark the faint lamp-beam on the kennell'd mud,
And listen to the drowsy cry of Watchmen
(Those hoarse unfeather'd Nightingales of Time!),
How many wretched Bards address thy name,
And hers, the full-orb'd Queen that shines above.
But I do hear thee, and the high bough mark,
Within whose mild moon-mellow'd foliage hid
Thou warblest sad thy pity-pleading strains.
O! I have listen'd, till my working soul,
Wak'd by those strains to thousand phantasies,
Absorb'd hath ceas'd to listen! Therefore oft,
I hymn thy name: and with a proud delight
Oft will I tell thee, Minstrel of the Moon!
'Most musical, most melancholy' Bird!
That all thy soft diversities of tone,
Tho' sweeter far than the delicious airs
That vibrate from a white-arm'd Lady's harp,
What time the languishment of lonely love
Melts in her eye, and heaves her breast of snow,
Are not so sweet as is the voice of her,
My Sara - best beloved of human kind!
When breathing the pure soul of tenderness,
She thrills me with the Husband's promis'd name!

The First Spring Day
Christina Rossetti (1830–94)

I wonder if the sap is stirring yet,
If wintry birds are dreaming of a mate,
If frozen snowdrops feel as yet the sun
And crocus fires are kindling one by one:
Sing, robin, sing;
I still am sore in doubt concerning Spring.

I wonder if the springtide of this year
Will bring another Spring both lost and dear;
If heart and spirit will find out their Spring,
Or if the world alone will bud and sing:
Sing, hope, to me;
Sweet notes, my hope, soft notes for memory.

The sap will surely quicken soon or late,
The tardiest bird will twitter to a mate;
So Spring must dawn again with warmth and bloom,
Or in this world, or in the world to come:
Sing, voice of Spring,
'Till I too blossom and rejoice and sing.

An Apple Gathering
Christina Rossetti (1830–94)

I plucked pink blossoms from mine apple-tree
And wore them all that evening in my hair:
Then in due season when I went to see
I found no apples there.

With dangling basket all along the grass
As I had come I went the selfsame track:
My neighbours mocked me while they saw me pass
So empty-handed back.

Lilian and Lilias smiled in trudging by,
Their heaped-up basket teased me like a jeer;
Sweet-voiced they sang beneath the sunset sky,
Their mother's home was near.

Plump Gertrude passed me with her basket full,
A stronger hand than hers helped it along;
A voice talked with her through the shadows cool
More sweet to me than song.

Ah Willie, Willie, was my love less worth
Than apples with their green leaves piled above?
I counted rosiest apples on the earth
Of far less worth than love.

So once it was with me you stooped to talk
Laughing and listening in this very lane:
To think that by this way we used to walk
We shall not walk again!

I let my neighbours pass me, one and twos
And groups; the latest said the night grew chill,
And hastened: but I loitered, while the dews
Fell fast I loitered still.

A Golden Day

Paul Laurence Dunbar (1872–1906)

I found you and I lost you,
All on a gleaming day.
The day was filled with sunshine,
And the land was full of May.
A golden bird was singing
Its melody divine,
I found you and I loved you,
And all the world was mine.
I found you and I lost you,
All on a golden day,
But when I dream of you, dear,
It is always brimming May.

Picture Credits

1, 104–105 John William Godward (1861–1922) *Choosing*, 1907 © Fine Art Photographic Library/SuperStock

3, 122 Sir Lawrence Alma-Tadema (1836–1912) *The Year's at the Spring, All's Right with the World*, 1902 © Fine Art Photographic Library/SuperStock

4 Dante Gabriel Rossetti (1828–1882) *The Bower Meadow*, 1872 © DeAgostini/SuperStock

7 John William Godward (1861–1922) *The Toilet*, 1900 © Christie's Images Ltd – ARTOTHEK

9 John William Waterhouse (1849–1917) *Vanity*, c. 1910 © Christie's Images Ltd./SuperStock

10–11 Sir Lawrence Alma-Tadema (1836–1912) *Expectations*, 1885 © Bridgeman Art Library, London/SuperStock

13 John William Waterhouse (1849–1917) *The Soul Of The Rose*, 1908 © Christie's Images Ltd./SuperStock

15 Sir Edward John Poynter (1836–1919) *Lesbia with Her Sparrow*, 1907 © Christie's Images Ltd – ARTOTHEK

18 John William Godward (1861–1922) *Dancer with Tambourine*, 1902 © Fine Art Images/SuperStock

21 Sir Lawrence Alma-Tadema (1836–1912) *Thou Rose of All the Roses*, 1883 © Fine Art Photographic Library/SuperStock

23 Sir John Everett Millais (1829–1896) *Il Penseroso* © Bridgeman Art Library, London/SuperStock

25 John William Waterhouse (1849–1917) *Undine*, 1872 © Image Asset Management Ltd./SuperStock

27 Sir Edward John Poynter (1836–1919) *Reading*, 1871 © Christie's Images Ltd – ARTOTHEK

28 Sir John Everett Millais (1829–1896) *Effie Deans*, 1877 © Christie's Images Ltd./SuperStock

32–33 Sir John Everett Millais (1829–1896) *Ophelia*, 1851-52 © Westermann – ARTOTHEK

34 John William Waterhouse (1849–1917) *Cleopatra*, 1888 © Christie's Images Ltd./SuperStock

37 John William Waterhouse (1849–1917) *Destiny*, 1900 © Bridgeman Art Library, London/SuperStock

38 Sir Lawrence Alma-Tadema (1836–1912) *Silver Favourites*, 1903 © Buyenlarge/SuperStock

41 Dante Gabriel Rossetti (1828–1882) *La Ghirlandata*, 1873 © Bridgeman Art Library, London/SuperStock

42–43 Sir Lawrence Alma-Tadema (1836–1912) *Ask Me No More*, 1906 © Image Asset Management Ltd./SuperStock

45 Sir Lawrence Alma-Tadema (1836–1912) *Coign of Vantage*, 1895 © Bridgeman Art Library, London/SuperStock

46 John William Godward (1861–1922) *Nerissa*, 1906 © Bridgeman Art Library, London/SuperStock

49 Sir Lawrence Alma-Tadema (1836–1912) *Quiet Greeting*, 1889 © Buyenlarge/SuperStock

52–53 John William Godward (1861–1922) *The Betrothed*, 1892 © Bridgeman Art Library, London /SuperStock

55 John Collier (1850–1935) *Portrait of the Artist's Wife Marian Huxley in her Wedding Dress*, 1880 © Christie's Images Ltd./SuperStock

57 Edmund Blair Leighton (1853–1922) *The Love Letter*, 1884 © Christie's Images Ltd./SuperStock

58 Sir John Everett Millais (1829–1896) *The Crown of Love*, 1875 © Fine Art Photographic Library/SuperStock

61 Arthur Hughes (1832–1915) *You Cannot Barre Love Oute*, 1870 © Fine Art Photographic Library/SuperStock

64–65 John William Waterhouse (1849–1917) *Boreas (Personification of the Wintery North Wind)* © Christie's Images Ltd – ARTOTHEK

66 John William Godward (1861–1922) *The New Perfume*, 1914 © Christie's Images Ltd./SuperStock

69 Edmund Blair Leighton (1853–1922) *Kissing*, 1903 © Fine Art Images/SuperStock

71 Sir Lawrence Alma-Tadema (1836–1912) *Expectation or Impatience* © Fine Art Photographic Library/SuperStock

73 Henry Treffry (1838–99) *Lady Lilith* © Christie's Images Ltd – ARTOTHEK

76–77 Edmund Blair Leighton (1853–1922) *The End Of The Song*, 1902 © Christie's Images Ltd./SuperStock

79 Sir John Everett Millais (1829–1896) *Sweet Emma Moreland*, 1892 © Fine Art Photographic Library/SuperStock

81 John William Waterhouse (1849–1917) *The Crystal Ball*, 1902 © Christie's Images Ltd./SuperStock

82–83 John William Godward (1861–1922) *The Favourite*, 1901 © Fine Art Photographic Library/SuperStock

85, 160 John William Godward (1861–1922) *Flowers of Venus*, 1890 © Christie's Images Ltd./SuperStock

87 Sir Frederic Leighton (1830–1896) *Type of Beauty* © Christie's Images Ltd – ARTOTHEK

90–91 Sir Frederic Leighton (1830–1896) *Greek Girl Dancing*, 1867 © Christie's Images Ltd./SuperStock

93 Sir Edward John Poynter (1836–1919) A Hot-House Flower, 1909 © Christie's Images Ltd – ARTOTHEK

95 Edmund Blair Leighton (1853–1922) *A Favour*, 1898 © Christie's Images Ltd – ARTOTHEK

96 Sir Frederick Leighton (1830–1896) *Portrait Of A Young Lady, Small Bust Length Wearing White Dress*, 19th century © Christie's Images Ltd./SuperStock

99 John William Godward (1861–1922) *Tender Thoughts*, 1917 © Christie's Images
Ltd./SuperStock

101 John William Godward (1861–1922) *Lucilia*, 1917 © Christie's Images Ltd – ARTOTHEK

107 John William Godward (1861–1922) *Cestilia*, 1919 © Christie's Images Ltd./SuperStock

110-11 Sir John Everett Millais (1829–1896) *Pot Pourri*, 1856 © Bridgeman Art Library,
London/Superstock

115 Sir John Everett Millais (1829–1896) *Portrait of Mrs. Joseph Chamberlain, Seated Three-
quarter Length at a Tea-table, Wearing a Grey and White Dress*, 1891 © Christie's Images
Ltd./SuperStock

116-17 Sir Lawrence Alma-Tadema (1836–1912) *Xanthe and Phaon*, 1883 © Fine Art
Photographic Library/SuperStock

119 John William Godward (1861–1922) *A Fair Reflection*, 1915 © Fine Art Images/SuperStock

121 Dante Gabriel Rossetti (1828–1882) *Reverie*, 1868 © Christie's Images Ltd./SuperStock

125 John William Godward (1861–1922) *A Roman Beauty*, c.1889 © Christie's Images Ltd –
ARTOTHEK

127 Sir Frederic Leighton (1830–1896) *Antigone*, 1882 © Christie's Images Ltd – ARTOTHEK

130-31 John William Godward (1861–1922) *Dolce Far Niente*, 1904 © Bridgeman Art
Library, London/SuperStock

134-35 John William Waterhouse (1849–1917) *The Awakening of Adonis*, 1899 © Christie's
Images Ltd – ARTOTHEK

138-39 John William Godward (1861–1922) *The Bouquet*, 1889 © Christie's Images Ltd –
ARTOTHEK

142-43 Sir Lawrence Alma-Tadema (1836–1912) *Woman Laying on Marble Bench*, 1901 ©
Fine Art Images/SuperStock

145 John William Godward (1861–1922) *A Song Without Words*, c. 1918 © Christie's Images
Ltd – ARTOTHEK

147 Edmund Blair Leighton (1853–1922) *The Cliff Path*, 1893 © Christie's Images Ltd - ARTOTHEK

150-51 John William Godward (1861–1922) *Tranquility*, 1914 © Fine Art Photographic
Library/SuperStock

153 John William Godward (1861–1922) *Cleonice*, 1913 © Christie's Images Ltd – ARTOTHEK

157 Sir Lawrence Alma-Tadema (1836–1912) *Summer Offering*, 1911 © Bridgeman – ARTOTHEK

158 Sir Frederic Leighton (1830–1896) *Odalisque*, 1862 © Christie's Images Ltd – ARTOTHEK

Indexes